Reverse Dog Training
A Fresh Perspective for Solving Common Problems

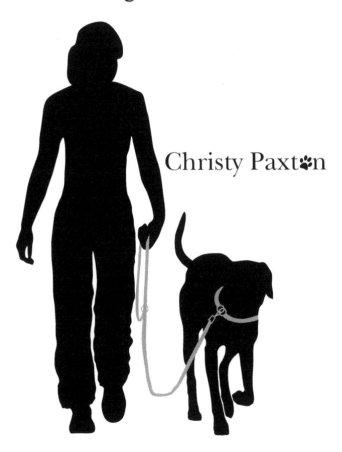

Christy Paxton

DEDICATION

This book is for all the dogs that want so badly to be understood. I dedicate it to my current dog, the Wonder Dog Tawny, who made me a better trainer, and especially to Jaspar, who is the reason I became a trainer. For all 17 years of his life, Jaspar tried to tell me what was wrong, and no matter how I tried, I could not understand. He's been gone for 10 years, and this book is for him especially. Jaspar, I finally got it!

This book is for all the humans who want so badly to understand their dogs. It is also for those humans who believed in me and supported me through this process. My family, in particular Mom. All my friends who listened patiently to all my passionate dog blather. And all the loving owners who allowed me the privilege of working with their precious pooches.

ACKNOWLEDGEMENT

Photographs created by Creed Woodka Photography,
http://www.creedwoodkaphotography.com/,
216-577-2486.

DISCLAIMER

Hand in Paw is registered in the state of Ohio as a sole proprietor, for-profit dog training business owned and operated by Christy Paxton. It is in no way affiliated with any other Hand in Paw company, business or organization, either for-profit or non-profit.

Contents

Introduction

In the classic TV series "Seinfeld," one typically hilarious episode has perennial loser George suddenly realizing that everything he'd done in his life had been wrong. To rectify his situation, he started doing the opposite of everything he would normally do, and bang! – great things and success rained down upon him. Ultimately, he used the method to score his dream job with the New York Yankees.

As odd as it may sound, I believe many dog owners are like the pre-opposite George. They are trying to train their dogs as best they can, as they always have, using what they think are the "right" things to do, either because they have always done things a certain way, or someone told them that's what they should do, or they read a book or watched a TV program, or because they think of the dogs as furry humans. Unfortunately, these assumptions can cause confusion, struggle and failure, often resulting in dogs being re-homed, returned and, sometimes, sadly, euthanized.

It's not only that these earnest owners – who generally love their dogs and want to do what's best – are using the wrong methods based on erroneous information, it's that in many cases, they are doing the _exact opposite_ of what they should be doing. Worse yet, when it doesn't work, they keep right on doing it, hoping, I suppose, that at some point it will sink into the dog's brain and behavior will finally change. To them, it's the dog that has the problem: "What is wrong with this dog?" wails the owner as he yells "OFF!" or "NO!" for the thousandth time. "Why doesn't he get it?"

Here's my first chance to show you want I mean by reverse dog training. It's not that the dog can't get it, it's that the owner isn't *giving* it properly. Your dog doesn't have a comprehension problem; you have a communication problem. You are speaking English, but your dog needs to hear Dog to get it.

Of course, this makes perfect sense when you hear it put that way, but it can be confusing when you try applying that statement to the problems you're having.

That's where this book comes in handy. It's chock full of new information and effective techniques that will help you do just that. For many of you, it will be a sea change in thinking, a total reversal in many cases of what you may be doing right now with your dog.

The best part: It works when the old stuff doesn't. Bonus: It's kinder, gentler, and more fun!

To give you a glimpse into what I mean, I invite you to take this short quiz. For each troublesome behavior listed, pick which action(s) you would take to deal with them:

Jumping
 A: Say Off/Down/No
  Push dog down
  Knee in chest/chin
  Grab/squeeze front paws while slowly lowering to ground
  Turn your back on dog
  Walk away
 B: Ignore
  Move toward jump
  Praise when four feet are on floor

Fear
  A: Comfort dog with "It's OK," petting, snuggling, etc.
  B: Ignore fear
    Pet/praise when calms down
Separation anxiety
  A: Give lots of attention
    Get a really strong crate
    Get another dog
    Play the TV/radio
  B: Decrease amount of attention given
Growl at child
  A: Strong No
    Smack on nose
    Banish
  B: Feed treats when child is near
    Invite dog to join you and child when calm
Lunges on leash
  A: Jerk/Yank leash
    Strong No
    Walk at night
  B: No reaction; turn dog away and reward when calm
Any unwanted behavior
  A: Yell No
    Yell name with authority
    Yank/pull/hold back on leash
  B: Laugh

How many As did you pick? If it was more than none, you are the people this book is really for. All the A options are incorrect; they are in fact the things you should never do because they can actually make the problems worse. To truly fix these problems, you want to use the B options. You will notice that most of these are the polar opposite of what you think would work!

If you picked all Bs, congratulations! You are well on your way to training success. I hope this book will expand your knowledge base.

This book is meant only as a guide full of general advice, and it is certainly not intended to replace sessions with a qualified, experienced trainer. If you are struggling with your dog, find someone in your area to work with who will help you reach your goals. For tips on how to find that someone, read the article on my Web site at ***http://www.cp-hipdogs.com (under "Resources").***

PART ONE

Reversing Basic Philosophies
(aka Myth Busting)

Don't agree. Yes, be kind but need to be good

Throughout my training career, I have been amazed at the over-the-top behavior of some of my students as they attempt to "show dominance" over their dogs. If I never hear the terms "pack leader" and "alpha dog" again, it will be too soon. I'm not saying anyone starts out planning to be mean to his/her dog. But I have seen some of the nicest, sweetest people in the world turn into militaristic boot-camp sadists when they start handling their dogs because someone told them they had to "be the boss" or "get tough" with their dogs so they will "respect you."

Good lord. Do you respect bullies? Do you like being pushed around, intimidated, frightened on a daily basis? Of course not! And neither does your dog!

These well-meaning owners are operating under the assumption that they are doing the right things to get an obedient dog, but their assumption is 100 percent wrong. There are many well-circulated statements out there that are taken as gospel but which are flat-out untrue, counterproductive, not very nice and even potentially dangerous to humans and/or dogs. Training has changed dramatically over the last 10 to 15 years, and it's much kinder, simpler (though not necessarily easier!) and more effective than ever before. Gone are the days of pinning down your dog, grabbing him by the scruff of the neck, smacking him with news-papers, and yanking his head off with a choke chain. You don't have to do any of that to achieve great results with any dog. **Any dog.** That includes aggressives, biters, leash crazies, and any other problem dog you can think of. You don't need to get tough with any of them to fix your problems.

Though a lot of this great information has been around for years, many owners have not been exposed to it. Longtime dog owners do not know about this because heck, they've had dogs and dogs, and they know how to handle them, like they've always done – until it doesn't work. Others watch "The Dog Whisperer" and, despite the repeated warnings on the show not to try these things on your own, they try these things on their own. And then people like me are brought in to clean up the mess.

So let me share some of this good stuff with you so you can start right now – today – to turn your human-dog relationship around and make it the best it can be.

First off, I'll tackle some general beliefs many owners embrace.

* * *

DOG'S MIND

COMMON BELIEF: *I've had dogs my whole life. I understand how my dog's mind works.*

REVERSE REALITY: Most people haven't a clue how a dog's mind works. They typically use old thinking (dogs are like wolves; they can "turn"; you have to show them who's boss), old methods (newspaper on the nose;

putting them on their backs; yelling in their face), and they usually humanize ("he knows it's wrong"; "he's being stubborn"; "she did it because she's mad at me"). These are all completely wrong assumptions and great contributors to training failures.

COMMON BELIEF: *My dog "knows" when he's doing "wrong."*

REVERSE REALITY: There is no moral code in the dog's world. They do not share our value system and do not use it to make decisions. So, dogs don't know right from wrong or good from bad.

COMMON BELIEF: *I can tell my dog knows what he's doing is "wrong" because he looks "guilty," even before I say or do anything.*

REVERSE REALITY: Since dogs have no sense of "right" or "wrong," they certainly can't experience guilt over doing something they shouldn't. What your dog does "know" is he should repeat behaviors that work for him (e.g. tearing up pillows is fun and relieves stress!). He also knows you are mad when you come in with your mad face and talk in your mad voice ("What did you do?!"), so he offers appeasement gestures (the "guilty" look) to you in hopes you will calm down and stop being so threatening.

Owners will often assume the dog "knows" because he will often slink away the moment you come in, before you even discover the indiscretion. That "pre-reaction" does not come from realizing he's committed a crime; rather, it comes from learning. Dogs know only the present, not the past or future, but they can learn.

That process goes something like this: "Every time Mom comes home and there is a torn pillow on the floor, she is mad and bad things happen to me, so I better do my best to calm her down/get out of here till she calms down."

Unfortunately, the dog cannot make the connection that if he hadn't destroyed the pillow in the first place, the bad things wouldn't happen.

Helpful side note: When your dog looks "guilty," he could actually be scared. NEVER correct a dog when he is scared.

COMMON BELIEF: *My dog does things just to get my goat/because he's mad at me.*

REVERSE REALITY: Dogs do things to get things (see "What are a dog's Precious Things?"), not to drive you crazy (though it does seem that way sometimes!). And as for seeking revenge, look at it this way: If you are a dog, and I come up and poke you in the eye, are you going to lay in wait, pick your moment, and tear up my favorite pair of shoes to get back at me? Of course not! You are going to bite me then and there, and rightly so, because I just poked you in the eye. Dogs truly live in the moment. Do they get frustrated? Yes, they do. But they are destroying your possessions for a very different reason than being mad at you. (See "Separation Anxiety" for more.)

COMMON BELIEF: *To properly communicate with my dog, all I need are commands.*

REVERSE REALITY: Commands do little good if they exist in isolation, especially when you are dealing with problems and/or difficult dogs. Many owners have told me, "He knows all his commands and all these tricks, but":

"...he won't come when called"

"...he still growls at my baby/spouse/ other dog"

"...he won't let anyone in the house"

"...he barks his head off"

"...he tears up my things"

etc., etc., etc.

Commands are not enough!

Commands are tools that help you shape your dog's behavior. If they only stand alone ("Look, my dog can sit!"), they are nothing more than parlor tricks. Commands, used properly when problems occur, are what will eventually change your dog's habits and give you the results you want.

Example: Your dog may have a "robo-sit," i.e., he will give you a sit under almost any circumstances. You look at him, and he plants his butt. Great! What are you using it for? Street corners? Before the front door opens? To have him earn a treat or toy? Not bad. But how about saying it right before someone approaches to prevent jumping? What about asking for it when he is agitated to help him calm down and focus? Now you are using commands to shape behavior.

What you need most is a basic understanding of how your dog's mind works so you can communicate properly with her.

DOMINANCE

COMMON BELIEF: *It's all about dominance.*

REVERSE REALITY: It has nothing to do with dominance, at least not in the way most people define it. This theory has been debunked, disproved and thrown out the window by everyone who is paying attention. Sorry, all you macho types who want to show the dog who's boss, this physically intimidating approach is scary for your dog, and it may cause him to defend himself against you or others. Pinning a dog down is a good way to get bitten and does not occur in nature.

Helpful side note: The study that all this nonsense was originally based on was a old, small one about wolves. When the study was reexamined, they found the conclusions to be wrong. It is now believed the wolves always OFFER appeasement postures like rollovers, and such postures are **NEVER FORCED UNLESS THE WOLF IS GOING TO BE KILLED.** *Yikes.* (See "Pack" section for more.)

COMMON BELIEF: *The way to show my dog who's boss is by eating first, walking through doors first, not allowing him on furniture, etc.*

REVERSE REALITY: Leadership comes from trust and cooperation between human and dog, not ritualistic displays like those above. Dogs want what they want, and of course they want a good place to sleep, all the food and toys they can get, and so on. Asking them to earn these things from you on an ongoing basis by doing things for you sets the cooperative and responsive tone you want.

You want to be a benevolent leader, ready to share all on a moment's notice, just as soon as you get a behavior you like.

Thinking that way, there really is no need for on-going displays. I think of the relationship more like a pick-up baseball game. Ever play a pick-up game? Who controls the game? The kid who brought the bat and the ball. Does it matter whose bat and ball it is when you are playing? No. It only matters occasionally (like when he has to go home for dinner). Otherwise, it's never mentioned or thought about. That's the leadership concept you want to use with your dog.

COMMON BELIEF: *My dog stares at me all the time. He's trying to dominate me. So I stare back to get him to look away first. I also will "stare him down" when he is doing something "wrong" to show him who's boss.*

REVERSE REALITY: Staring between dogs is not a dominance exercise; it is a fight challenge. We don't want them thinking we are picking fights with them! Unfortunately, humans tend to stare endlessly into dogs' eyes: to try to dominate them, but also when we try to be friendly (can't imagine why that would confuse them!). What person doesn't lock eyes and say "Hi Sparky!" when greeting a dog, and then is puzzled when the dog looks away, moves away, ducks when we reach for him, jumps at our face or even growls or snaps? Hmmm, wonder why that happens? Could it be we are making the dog uncomfortable with our human overtures?

Continually staring at a dog can actually create or re-inforce insecurity, whether you are trying to intimidate them or not. If you have an insecure dog, she might stare at you a lot. (My dog Tawny does this. I call her my stalker dog.) You may think it's because she loves you (I'm sure she does, but that's not what this is about). If you constantly meet that stare (which you do, because we humans have a condition called "auto dog eye-lock"), you end up reinforcing the anxiety every time you do. It's like that insecure person we all know who needs constant validation. But she never feels more secure.

Reverse your dog's attitude toward eye contact with humans by:

Not staring. *Look, and look away, then look back. Smile and crinkle those eyes up. Relax and blink, for heaven's sake! It's social and non-threatening.*

Play the eye contact game. *Show the dog a treat, then sweep it up to your eyes. When she looks at the treat, she also meets your gaze. Immediately praise and treat. Do that over and over, gradually increasing the time you hold the eye contact. Once your dog understands this game, have more people do it with her. You don't have to be close to her; if you aren't sure how she is with eye contact, stand several feet away, call her name happily, make kiss sounds, then when she looks, toss the treat to her. The more you play this game, the more she will realize that humans are not threatening her when they stare.*

PACK

Common belief: *It's all about pack. Dogs are pack animals, and I have to be pack leader/alpha dog through domination of my dogs.*

Reverse reality: Among the distinguished and various researchers in the dog world, there is no consensus as to whether dogs are pack animals. Ray and Lorna Coppinger ("Dogs: A Startling New Understanding of Canine Origin, Behavior and Evolution," 2001, New York: Scribner) make a compelling argument for the "village dog" concept, which puts early dogs at the edges of villages, as solitary figures, begging for scraps.

Long-term research on groups of dogs by Dr. Frank Beach show many differences in the structure of a dog group versus a wolf group. Structure is more fluid, for example, especially among females ("Alpha This Alpha That," by Maureen Ross, M.A., published in Dog Talk & TheraPet, LLC, June 2009).

Whether dogs are or aren't pack animals actually shouldn't be a big concern for owners because it really has little impact on the dog-owner relationship. Yes, you want structure and leadership for your group, pack or not. But what you are looking to create is an atmosphere of mutual respect and trust.

CORRECTION, REINFORCEMENT (POSITIVE, NEGATIVE)

Common belief: *Dogs have to be corrected whenever they do something "wrong."*

REVERSE REALITY: If you are defining correction as some kind of strong reaction to be delivered for any and all infractions, then no, they should not be corrected for every "wrong." Remember, dogs don't do "right" and "wrong" things, they do things we want them to do and things we don't want them to do. There is no intent on the part of the dog to "break the rules" or "get away with something." They simply repeat those behaviors that are paying off for them somehow.

A correction is not a punishment, and it should never be delivered in anger or with frustration. If you are doing that, you need to stop right now. You are not doing your dog or yourself any good, and in fact you may well be making the situation worse by putting way too much emphasis/energy/stress into trying to stop a "bad" behavior.

A correction is simply an interruption, something that says to the dog, "Hang on a second. Stop and wait for instructions." The energy devoted to that correction should be the barest minimum needed. What happens *after* that is much more important than the correction. You should never stop at No.

So instead of constantly identifying your dog's "wrong" behavior, start emphasizing what he is doing "right." Change the energy you are giving out from negative to positive, and change the emphasis from the "bad" (unacceptable) behavior to the "good" (acceptable) behavior you are going to get out of him. Maximum energy should be devoted to creating the new behavior and praising, loving, treating, etc. that dog to let her know how much you liked that new behavior.

Right about now, you are probably saying, "HUH? My dog is jumping all over me, biting me, eating my couch. I need to STOP THAT. He needs to know it's wrong. Right?"

Wrong. He needs to know you don't want him to give you THAT behavior, but much more importantly, he needs to know you want THIS behavior INSTEAD. This is tough, because we humans tend to be reactive rather than proactive, hence we tend to wait till something happens before we do anything about it instead of doing the preventive work that would keep it from happening in the first place (How many people *really* practice fire drills in their home?). The huge mistake many owners make (I've done it too) is putting every bit of energy, anger and frustration into stopping a behavior, when really the emphasis should be on starting a new behavior and rewarding substantially when they get it.

This is the basic concept behind positive reinforcement, which most owners believe they understand and use. Sadly, most owners understand very little about it. Happily, I explain it further below!

Helpful side note: Anyone who has ever associated with kids understands this statement: Sometimes any attention is good attention, even bad attention. Same applies to dogs – the payoff is there, so I'll take it. It worked for me (made you look!), so I'll do it again. So don't let it work for them! Make sure the only thing that "works" for them is the behavior you want.

COMMON BELIEF: *I understand positive reinforcement. My dog sits, I treat and say "Good dog." That's it.*

REVERSE REALITY: Not even close! You are sitting on a gold mine, and all you are looking at is the dust on top.

If you are constantly saying No and working to stop "bad" behaviors, you haven't a clue about what positive reinforcement (PR) really means. Stopping at No or a correction is not positive, is it? You are not using the tools you have to shape behavior and get what you want. All you are doing is waiting for your dog to mess up. How positive is that?

When you stop at No/correction, you are not done because you have not told your dog what the "good" behavior is that he can get rewarded for. You have only stated half the sentence, and you have left out the most important part.

You must TEACH your dog the acceptable behavior, ask for it over and over, and reward mightily when you get it. Then whenever he gives you the unacceptable behavior, react with a tsk-tsk/silly-you casualness, and ask him for the acceptable behavior you taught him. If he doesn't give it to you right away, help him by reminding him great rewards are pending (see this hot dog, pal?), and when he finally does it, lavish! Now we are talking real positive reinforcement. You have successfully used it to shape behavior.

Helpful side note: Dogs' goal in life is not to dominate, but to get stuff. Specifically, stuff they consider important. I call this stuff Precious Things. Dogs will work very hard to get them.

If you know this about them, you can use this knowledge to train them. Simply put: When your dog does what you want, you give her Precious Things. When she doesn't, you don't.

What are a dog's Precious Things?
Anything the dog desires. Food, of course. But plenty of other things: attention (which includes looking at them and talking to them), petting, kisses, snuggles, hugs, playing, toys, outside, car rides, walks, etc. etc. etc. You may have some special ones for your own dog. My dog Tawny loves sniffing – me, outside, practically anything (no, she is not part Beagle!). So for Tawny, sniffing is a Precious Thing, and I use it to train her. For example, when I first got her, she used to jump all over me and generally act like an idiot when I came home. To change her behavior, I took away her Precious Things: I ignored her (attention removed) and didn't allow her to approach and sniff me. Then I went about my business and waited until the jumping stopped and the idiotic behavior went away. When that happened, I returned her Precious Things – I greeted her and let her give me a thorough sniff to find out where I've been (and how many dogs I've been with!).

Essentially, I corrected her jumping/idiot behavior by withdrawing anything she considers good, worthwhile, a payoff – I gave her absolutely nothing until I saw a behavior I wanted. (By the way, this is what I call a correction.) And then she got everything she wanted!

Compare this to what most people due to deal with jumping: They jump back, yell "NO!" or "OFF!" or "DOWN!" and push the dog away. He continues jumping; owners continue yelling and pushing. It doesn't work; owners get mad and therefore louder and more demonstrative, say pointing at him and yelling, "Knock it off! There's no jumping! No jumping! Now stop it!" When he finally does stop for whatever reason, owners mutter, "Thank God" and go about their business.

In that scenario, which behavior paid off better for the dog? For jumping, he got lots of attention and physical contact. For not jumping, he got…nothing. Which behavior are owners likely to see again? Reverse your reaction, and you will get the opposite result. (See "Jumping" for more.)

Let's take a different behavior.

Say your dog is barking his head off at the front window (Tawny!). You scream "Quiet!" which doesn't work, then come charging into the room and chase your dog away from the window. You return to what you were doing muttering, "Stupid dog. Why won't he shut up?" Next thing you know, he's back at it again.

For barking, he got lots of attention and a chase game. For not barking, he got…nothing. (See "Barking" for more.)

> *Grasping the real meaning of PR is often difficult for many owners, and I believe it's because they tend to be reactive instead of proactive. In other words, they don't plan ahead. To help you get going, I suggest writing down all your dog's bad habits, then what you would like him to do instead ("nothing" is an acceptable answer too, by the way!). Then start teaching him those new habits today and reward mightily whenever you see one. Then you will have something to ask him for the next time the old bad habit appears.*
>
> *This all takes time, so be patient with yourself. (Your dog will catch on faster than you, trust me!)*

COMMON BELIEF: *Treats are bribes. My dog should do things for me just to please me.*

REVERSE REALITY: A bribe is something you receive before you do something. Treats are delivered *after* your dog does something for you – the opposite of a bribe.

Treats are motivators, rewards. They are the prizes the dog wins when they play the training game the right way. The only reason dogs do things "to please me" during the training phase is because they hope they will then get what they want – in this case, the TREAT!

You don't have to use treats, but if you don't, you generally have to work a lot harder or longer to get the results you want. Sometimes old-school harsh methods are also employed to make sure the dog does what will please the owner.

Of course, you don't want to use treats forever. But this is training, after all. The biggest motivator comes at the beginning of the process (FOOD), when the dog needs the most support. When you are getting the behavior you want reliably, then you gradually wean the dog off treats and REPLACE them with a different Precious Thing (e.g. attention, petting, praise, snuggles, car rides, walks, play time, special toys, etc. etc. etc.; see "What are a dog's Precious Things?").

There is science behind this. I am no scientist, so I will utilize the expertise of someone who knows something about science and is also a fantastic trainer, Patricia McConnell. In her book, "For the Love of a Dog: Understanding Emotion in You and Your Best Friend" (2007; New York: Ballantine Books/Random House) she explains that the treat gives us access to the limbic system, a primitive part of the brain, thus allowing us to connect great pleasure with doing things for us. It's actually the smell that makes the connection, which is why you want to use nice, smelly treats. Once that connection is established, then you can start to back off on the highest-level payoff (food). Gradually. The goal here is to allow the dog to hold out hope that there is a treat coming at some point, and that he will continue to perform with that hope intact. Sort of like a gambler who hits one jackpot on the slots, then pulls that handle over and over in hopes of hitting another. It's a concept called sporadic reinforcement, and it works with humans and dogs.

Helpful side note: Some owners get very frustrated when using treats because they either forget or do not know how to progress the exercise and wean off the treats. Showers of treats at the beginning gradually give way to a light rain, a sprinkle, and then gone (except for those great, sporadic jackpots!). Once the dog understands what's expected, then the treats are stretched out/used less. Most owners forget to do that, maintaining the exercise/reward rate exactly the same. When the frustration sets in, they often then drop treats completely, further frustrating themselves and the dog, who has no clue what he did to stop the gravy train.

Example: Walking is a primary complaint/struggle area. My basic walking exercise is, walk beside me on a loose leash, and I will feed you. So, I show the food to the dog, ask her to follow it for a few steps, then I stop and deliver the treat. Once the dog is focused on that treat and has this exercise cold, then I start asking for five steps, six, seven, eight before the treat is given. Then the treat starts to disappear for awhile – show it, hide it, show it, hide it, feed. Hide it for longer periods of time, start paying the food out from a pocket instead of your hand. Eventually, the food doesn't come out anymore. But all the while, I'm substituting my voice for the food, as well as other things like sniff time, pee time, run time, play time, etc. Walking in a straight line for long distances and doing nothing else is a completely foreign, and I'm sure ridiculous, concept to a dog. So they need a lot of convincing that this is worthwhile before they will do it without payoff!

Helpful side note: Watch out for treat manipulation! This is another area of frustration for owners, and it is also caused by non-progression of the exercise. I'll go back to walking as an example: To encourage attention, you treat every time the dog looks at you. Pretty soon, he learns to look at you every time he wants a treat, and otherwise does his own thing. If he looks away right after getting the treat, that is treat manipulation. Next time it happens, sneak away in another direction and praise when he follows; repeat every time he looks away.

COMMON BELIEF: *"Tough" dog breeds need tougher handling than most. You really need to show them who's boss!*

REVERSE REALITY: My experience is that those "tough" dogs – bull terriers, Rottweilers, bulldogs, boxers, Dobermans, etc. – need a very calm and gentle hand, almost more so than other breeds. These dogs are generally intelligent, sensitive, insecure and overreactive. They wear their hearts on their sleeves – they get REALLY HAPPY! or REALLY ANXIOUS! or REALLY FOCUSED! or REALLY FRUSTRATED! Everything comes out big. People often misinterpret these reactions and, instead of constructively working to focus and calm the dogs – to teach them how to calm themselves down – owners jump in with the strong corrections that end up pouring gasoline on the fire, essentially making the reaction worse by giving it so much attention in an attempt to stop it.

SOCIALIZATION/PLAY/GETTING ALONG

COMMON BELIEF: *I can't play tug with my dog because it can cause aggression.*

REVERSE REALITY: Tug is a marvelous game to play with your dog as long as you do it right. It is a wonderful training tool, and it can help redirect a natural behavior (prey drive).

The rules are: You start and end the game (true of any game, by the way), they must let go when you say so, and if any teeth touch flesh, game is over.

That's it! Now tug away.

COMMON BELIEF: *Taking my dog to dog parks and doggie daycares from a young age will prevent her from becoming aggressive. This is socialization.*

REVERSE REALITY: Just because dogs are around other dogs and play with other dogs doesn't mean they are socialized. And it certainly doesn't stop dog-dog aggression from developing. I've seen a fair number of dogs that have done just fine in these places early in life suddenly ejected once adolescence/early adulthood kicks in.

Well-socialized dogs are ones that behave the same way (i.e. well) in a variety of situations. To socialize your dog, you need to thoughtfully expose early and often to as many people, places and things as possible so nothing is new, strange and scary. Dogs don't all have to love each other (heaven knows people don't either!) and play well with each other, but they need to behave around each other and be polite.

Dog parks and doggie daycares certainly have their place, but just like human playgrounds, they need rules that are followed by both dogs and owners, and they need plenty of supervision to make sure those rules are followed. Any dog going into these places should have, at the very least, a great Come and an Emergency Recall (if Come fails) to get him out of any situations he shouldn't be in. I would also like to see a Leave it, an Enough, a Watch/Look at me and a Let's go/Heel so you have as many tools as possible to use to get your dog to respond. It also wouldn't hurt to be able to read some dog body language so you can head off trouble before it blows up into something big. (Turid Rugaas' "On Talking Terms with Dogs - Calming Signals," 2nd ed. [2006; Wenatchee, WA: Dogwise Publishing] is a little book but a great big resource that outlines dozens of different social signals dogs send out that most owners have no clue about.)

Helpful side note: An *Emergency Recall* can get your dog out of a lot of trouble. The Come command will fail sometimes (dogs aren't perfect!), so it's good to have a Plan B when it does. (See **COME** in **Section Two** for tips on how to teach it.)

Common belief: *Dogs need to interact/play with other dogs to be happy.*

Reverse reality: While it's really fun to see your dog cavorting with her own kind, I don't put a lot of emphasis on this because they spend most of their time with us, and I believe they really like us as much or more than other dogs. Yes, they are social creatures, but I feel the emphasis should be on lots of interaction with humans so their tolerance level of our miscommunications with them is as high as possible (so they will, for example, turn away or walk away from a child pulling their ears rather than snap at him). Dogs have been domesticated for a long time, which means they have been hanging around us more than their own kind. Even before that, they may not have been hanging out all that much with their fellow pooches. Some researchers don't think they are pack animals but solitary surfers for the most part, "village dogs" that hung around our periphery making appeasement gestures they hoped would lead to scrap sharing (See "Pack" section).

My own dog has no interest in other dogs, except in her commitment to avoiding them or driving them off. Dogs actually scare her. When off leash, she avoids them; on leash, she used to charge them in an attempt to drive them away. I could speculate endlessly about why she is this way (she was a stray picked up at one or two years old), and work tirelessly to introduce her to new dog friends, but frankly, I don't care if she ever has a dog buddy unless I choose to add another dog to my family. She is happy, healthy, and not doing all the "bad things" she came to me with (trust me, there were a lot!). But let me be clear: I do care, very much, that she behaves herself while around other dogs, no matter how she feels about them. That's where my training effort goes.

Helpful side note: If your goal in life is to take your dog everywhere with you so you can hang out with your dog-owning friends, then of course you must care whether your dog plays nice with other dogs (see the previous references to daycares and dog parks). Your dog should be social with other dogs in that scenario so you don't have to keep him leashed/crated/muzzled while everyone else is running around free. But understand that some dogs are just not meant for play groups, and you may need to adjust your lifestyle if you find you have a dog like that. (Learn more about play and its relationship to training, etc. in the DVD "Dog Play: Understanding Play Between Dogs and Between Dogs and People" by Patricia McConnell [2009; McConnell Publishing Ltd.])

If you are not one to participate in human play groups much yourself, don't feel guilty if your dog doesn't do that either. You got a companion for you, not other dogs, right?

COMMON BELIEF: *Getting two dogs of the same age is a great idea – they grow up together, play together and keep each other company.*

REVERSE REALITY: Sometimes, this works out great. Other times, not. It goes badly when the dogs bond to each other instead of their owners, which renders the humans insignificant. The dogs can egg each other on (barking, escaping, destruction), making training harder. They can become destructively addicted to each other, resulting in particularly vicious dog fights. This happens often enough that it actually has a name: "Littermates Syndrome."

Think twice or thrice before saying "Make mine a double." If you decide to go ahead and get two, get one male and one female (male-male and female-female combos tend to be worse). Make it your mission to separate them early and often, train them separately, insist on polite behavior with each other at all times, and keep your eyes peeled for any signs of overreactive intolerance until they are at least two years old.

If you want two but don't care if they are the same age, go for dogs that are approximately a year apart in age. Their activity levels will be close, but the maturation hormones won't go off at the same time!

COMMON BELIEF: *Getting dogs of the same breed guarantees I'll get the same temperament (The "All (insert your breed here)s are the same" assumption).*

REVERSE REALITY: While certain breeds have certain temperament tendencies, your dog may not have or display such tendencies. (Appearance and temperament are somewhat related.) Reputable breeders will watch for temperament problems and work to weed them out of their gene pool. However, breeders' emphasis tends to be on appearance – a Doberman has to look like a Doberman, not a Golden Retriever – because most people want a certain look. Some soon-to-be-owners will order their dog in advance, specifying sex, color etc. Temperament is not always high on that list (or it's assumed it is just part of that breed). It becomes cross-your-fingers time that a decent personality comes with that look.

Assuming all Breed X dogs do that or don't do that may cause owners to miss problems developing and limit their success in training. During a workshop I held a couple of years ago for a Husky rescue group, an attendee commented she couldn't get good walking out of her dog because "Huskies pull." I replied, "Not in my class they don't." She had already concluded it couldn't work, so of course it didn't work.

I don't care the breed, the sex, the age, the history; you have to deal with the dog in front of you. What behaviors are you getting; what behaviors would you like instead; and how are you going to get there? Period. Do you have to make adjustments based on the dog you see? Of course. Might you have to work harder because of a breed tendency? Of course. But don't assume failure or you will get failure. Assume success and get to it!

COMMON BELIEF: *Getting a dog from a breeder who raises dogs on a farm is the best early environment for a puppy.*

REVERSE REALITY: Maybe, if you live on a farm too. But most dog owners live in places that are much less bucolic and more loud, rushed, and full of things that puppies don't experience in a farm environment.

I don't mean to trash reputable breeders, so let's be clear about what kind of farm we are talking about. Pay attention to the socialization the dog experienced there:

- Was he kenneled outside/in a separate building, or was he kept in the house?
- Did he have interaction with humans – all kinds – or mostly other dogs?
- How much time was allotted to taking the dog out and about to see the rest of the world during his early life?
- How clean was the environment?

The "farm" dogs I've treated for behavior problems have not been exposed to the lifestyle they are being put into. They were in a setting that had lots of quiet and few traffic sounds, screaming kids, motorcycles, etc. Some have never been in a house before, so they aren't aware of stairs, furniture, enclosed spaces (like hallways or cars), TVs, music, etc. etc. etc. In other words, they have been massively undersocialized, vastly increasing the possibility of fear/startle reactions in young dogs. Critical socialization periods happen young (ending at about 16 weeks), and those unaware of this can risk raising a jumpy dog if they don't get their dogs out and about early.

Breeders sometimes miss the early socialization period, or leave it up to the dogs to do it for them, misunderstanding the concept of socialization as being good with other dogs and not good with the world. Owners usually miss the later period because they don't know about it or they think it is more important to get all the shots before exposing them to the world. The reverse is also true here: It is SO MUCH MORE IMPORTANT to get a dog out to see the world so that it is less scary later than to worry about illness, in my view.

I'm not saying you can't get a good dog from a farm-based breeder, but you need to ask a few more questions to get a realistic picture of the dog's world and what you will have to do to transition her to your household and your life.

Helpful side note: Be sure to get your pup vet checked BEFORE bringing her home. It's not just the neglected dogs that have internal parasites, urinary tract infections and ear infections.

***

POSSIBILITIES

COMMON BELIEF: *My dog is not fixable. He is too old/too far gone, etc.*

REVERSE REALITY: Unless there is a medical problem, I firmly believe (and have proved through my own clients) that just about every problem is fixable with enough time and effort. I have seen crazy Cujo dogs turn into happy Buddha dogs. I have seen frozen-with-fear dogs thaw and live happily. I have seen anxiety dogs who tore up houses and themselves calm down and deal well with separation. And I have seen it in all ages, all breeds, all dogs.

That doesn't mean all dogs can be saved and kept in the original home. The owner may not be willing to put in the time and effort. The ultimate reverse reality here is that you will fix your dog by first changing yourself!

PART TWO

Reverse Problems by Reversing Techniques

Now that I've got your thinking turned around so you have a better understanding of how your dog works and what your impact is upon her, it's time to get into the specifics of how that basic change in thinking can help you solve those vexing problems many owners have.

This is certainly not comprehensive, and it is in no way intended to replace a good class or private training sessions with a quality trainer. My hope is that it will get your creative problem-solving juices flowing and serve as a great reference tool for you as you continue your training journey with your interesting, challenging, wonderful dog!

Important: Whenever dealing with a problem behavior, always err on the side of caution. If you get angry, stop. If you are uncertain as to the mood of your dog, stop. Even if you are sure you know what to do, if you think your dog is getting frustrated, scared, or otherwise overstimulated, stop. Never push your dog past his comfort level. It's not worth a bite to be right. Enlist the help of a qualified professional to get on the right track!

***

<u>ATTENTION, RESPONSIVENESS</u>

Yelling/Saying it "like you mean it"

COMMON BELIEF: *Yelling/Saying it "like you mean it" is a necessity. It's the only way I can get my dog to listen.*

REVERSE REALITY: Yelling/Saying it "like you mean it" is an intimidation tactic that only works when partnered with follow-through, which is what really makes things happen in training. If you say "No" five times to no response from your dog, then yell "NO!" and finally get up and do something about it, it is not the "NO!" part but the "doing something about it" part that is getting the dog to react. You are finally providing a consequence for the noncompliance. Get up after the first "no" and, not only do you not have to yell, you won't be mad or frustrated like you usually are when yelling, and you will be much better able to deal with the situation calmly and efficiently. Most importantly, you will be in a much better frame of mind, so you'll be able to *praise your dog when he stops what he's doing* (that's what No means – "Stop what you are doing." It's just another command). That's right, praise after No! If he's responding to this command (No), you *must* praise to reinforce the stopping. That way, you increase the odds he will stop again when you ask him to. Your dog did what you asked. So reward him!

Your dog reads you all the time – your body, your face, what your eyes are doing, if your jaw is set or relaxed, the tone of voice you are using. If you look and/or sound angry, the last thing he wants to do is look at you (not respectful in dog terms) or be near you

(you=mad; me=scared, outta here). By acting angry/ tough/intimidating, you are making it less likely your dog will respond to you the way you want him to.

> **DO:**
> *Use the same word in in the same way every time*
> *Use a normal tone for all commands*
> *Say it once, make it happen*
> *Deliver a consequence only for noncompliance*
> *Emphasize/reward the proper behavior even if it comes after No.*
>
> **DON'T:**
> *Yell*
> *Intimidate*
> *Use anger*
> *Stare down*

The word NO

COMMON BELIEF: *NO should always be said sternly, loudly, and without using the dog's name.*

REVERSE REALITY: Where to start with this chestnut? First of all, if you don't use his name, and he isn't looking at you, how does he know you are addressing him? If I have three people standing in front of me with their backs to me, and I yell "DUCK!" who should duck?

The dog needs an attention-getter (his name), followed by information. No is the information. It means stop what you are doing. It is a command, not a correction/punishment. So just like any other command, it should be delivered in a normal tone of voice and, when it is complied with (dog stops what he is doing), you should praise your dog. I do mine!

Helpful side note: If you have wrecked your No by turning it into something horrible and scary, retrain using "uh-uh" or "Stop" or similar as your stop-what-you-are-doing command. Keep it positive!

DO:
Say it once
Speak in normal tone
Use dog's name
Reward when compliant

DON'T:
Yell
Use anger

Repeating commands

COMMON BELIEF: *I have to keep repeating until my dog does what I want. How else can I get him to listen and respond?*

REVERSE REALITY: If you are repeating your dog's name and/or No and other commands (No is just another command; see above), first realize he *heard* you but is *not responding*. So the repeating is obviously not working. What you are doing is trying to nag your dog into compliance. Does nagging work with people? No. And it sure doesn't work with dogs, either. In fact, it has the opposite effect; repeating essentially renders a word meaningless. Saying a command once and then following through on making it happen, or delivering a consequence for noncompliance, teaches your dog that responding the first time is the thing to do because it gets him the best result.

Helpful side note: "Making it happen" and "delivering a consequence" are ways to help your dog complete the command. Example: My dog must sit calmly to be leashed. I present the leash and say "Sit." She does, but when I reach down to leash her, she pops up and starts dancing around. I stand back up and look away. She calms herself and eventually sits down again. When she does, I reach down again. Every time she gets up, I stand up and look away. If she gets too crazy, I drop the leash and walk away for a few minutes, then come back, pick up the leash, and stand there. Eventually, she will get the idea that the only way she is getting leashed and hopefully out the door for a walk is to stay seated through the leashing process. The consequence here is that you stop what you are doing and take your attention away from your dog (removing Precious Things) when she is not doing what you want. You make it happen not by saying Sit over and over, struggling to grab the collar, leash her up and get out the door, but by waiting her out, and only giving back the Precious Things when she is being compliant. Easy to say, hard to do – I speak from experience since patience was not my strong suit before becoming a trainer, and I still struggle with it!

Helpful side note: Make sure you are using your dog's name correctly. When you say "Sparky," all you are asking for is attention. Do not say it and expect your dog to look at you (unless you have taught him to do so); do not say it in an angry tone (as if it is another word for No/Stop what you are doing – the dog's name should always be wonderful and positive!); do not say it and expect your dog to Come. *Each word you teach your dog can have only one meaning.* The meaning of your dog's name is "Attention, please." Once you have it, tell him what you want!

DO:
Say it once, make it happen
Use a normal tone
Say name followed by information (what you want dog to do)

DON'T:
Use name as Come, Look at me or No
Use angry/stern tone
Use command without name (unless dog is looking at you)
Use name without command (unless you are teaching dog his name)

Happy voice!

COMMON BELIEF: *Using a "happy voice" is a good way to train my dog. It gets him really excited about training!*

REVERSE REALITY: The "happy voice" most people use and the "happy voice" that should be used for training and interacting with your dog are two entirely different things. I have dubbed the owners' version the "yappy happy," because frankly, it makes them sound like a bunch of unstable, overstimulated nut dogs when they use it. That high-pitched tone (produced more often by women than men, for obvious reasons) comes out of dogs when they are not exhibiting calmness and manners, and it is not something we want to emulate when we are trying to impress them with our leadership skills! I've actually seen that voice create jumps, mouthings, clothing grabs and nips, even a complete breakdown in training, all not the intended effect.

Bring that "Good dog!" out of the stratosphere and into the mid-range. Get "gooshy" with it, and draw out those vowels to calm ("Sparky's such a gooooooood booooooy"). Your dog will eat it up. You will know you've hit the right note if your dog stays in the same mood (e.g. remains laying calmly where he is instead of jumping up).

Helpful side note: You can also pet your dog to keep him calm by using long, slow, sweeping strokes instead of quick rubbing motions, which can rev up instead of calm down.

Helpful side note: Dogs are more visual than verbal, so concentrate on less talking and more showing (what is your face/body telling your dog?)!

> **DO:**
> *Use positive tone*
> *Match dog's energy*
> *Stretch vowels to calm*
> *Use as a reward to mark behavior*
>
> **DON'T:**
> *Use "yappy happy" tone*
> *Talk incessantly*

BARKING

COMMON BELIEF: *My dog will not stop barking. I've tried everything!*

REVERSE REALITY: Well, you haven't tried everything, because you haven't succeeded yet. Barking can be really aggravating, so the "everything" most owners have tried involves frustration-type corrections that can actually end up reinforcing the barking!

Before you try anything, let's redefine what you want. You don't want your dog to stop barking entirely; you do want him to stop when you ask him too. And it would be nice if he alert barked a little instead of doing that crazy-dog thing when the mailman approaches, or a dog walks by. Correct?

Next, you need to figure out WHY he is barking. There can be more than one cause here depending on when he is doing it (barking at you when you are watching TV versus, say, barking at a dog approaching on leash). Which means you may well need more than one solution.

Now, let's define "everything." I assume you mean you have yelled, screamed, yanked/dragged him away, thrown a can full of pennies at him, squirted him with water or other substances, and/or thrown him in his crate. So by "everything," you mean "everything that doesn't work and makes things worse."

The classic mistake here is your emphasis is on the wrong thing. You are doing everything you can to STOP the barking. You are putting all the energy into stopping that behavior. So how much attention is your dog getting for barking? LOTS. If she stops barking for whatever reason, how much attention does she get then? NONE.

So, reverse it: Put the emphasis on creating and rewarding the quiet, not stopping the barking.

DO:

Learn to recognize the different barks your dog uses to convey information (Mom's home! vs. Alert! vs. I want to go out! vs. Danger! vs. Squirrel!)

Teach Enough/Quiet so you have a positive thing to ask for and reward

Teach a great Come, Leave it and Watch to use to redirect

Wave a tasty treat in front of your dog's face and, when she realizes what it is and reaches for it, you guide her away from the focus of the barking/ask her to do something else, and feed the treat when you get it.

Interrupt the barking with sound (strange vocalization, clapping, etc.) and then enthusiastically say "Good dog!" followed by some other command or game that brings her away from the target and towards you.

Attach a leash and, every time she barks, draw her away (gentle tugs not yanks/drags) from the window/door/fence/room/outside/etc. Once she calms down, let her go back. Praise when she watches or listens quietly.

If on leash, start feeding treats to interrupt the barking and keep feeding till the target passes. If she stops eating, move farther away and try again. (If barking leads to a full-out leash frenzy, see **Leash aggression/ overreactivity.***)*

DON'T:
Yell from another room and not follow up
Get angry/frustrated
Correct every little bark. These are dogs. They bark.
Chase from room to room, window to window, in your house while they are barking

BITING (PUPPY NIPPING)

COMMON BELIEF: *The proper reaction to puppy nipping is a strong No and a tap on the nose. Possibly some yelling and pushing away if she really gets hold of me. Those teeth are sharp!*

REVERSE REALITY: Puppy biting is as common as rain in Hawaii, and owners struggle mightily with it. But you are not going to get rid of it by getting physical with your dog. She's already getting physical with you, so don't add to the problem!

Puppies will bite you in play, to get your attention, when they are being affectionate, and sometimes in an attempt to herd you. They don't have hands, so they use their mouths. We have to teach them it is never OK to put teeth or lips on human skin or clothing. But the way to do it is to let it extinguish by not giving the dog what she wants (attention, play, etc.). Yelling and interacting with her is really paying her off for what she's doing!

Kids are especially bad at dealing with this, so the adults need to take the lead and supervise them.

Helpful side note: Puppy biting usually fades away by the five- or six-month mark. If it hasn't, you may need some training help.

IMPORTANT: Puppy nipping is not the same as adult dogs or puppies displaying aggressive/guarding behavior. That is a much more serious issue. Do not attempt to deal with it yourself. Find a qualified professional to help you as soon as possible.

DO:

Spend more time praising her for 'good' behavior (like stopping biting or choosing to lick rather than bite) than you are correcting her for 'bad' behavior.

Make a CONVINCING pain sound (doesn't have to be loud just realistic) every time your dog puts her mouth on you. If you can do a puppy yelp, good; otherwise a realistic human pain sound is fine. Make the sound and freeze. Do NOT pull your hand away. Don't look mad or say no. She should be startled and stop. You can then reengage with her (all is forgiven). If she does it again, repeat as long as she is responsive to it. If it stops working, then stop engaging with her. She will learn if she bites, she loses your attention.

Teach her the "Kisses" command: Put a little peanut butter on the back of your hand and, as she licks it off, say, "Kisses, good girl," over and over. Then when she starts to mouth you even slightly, say, "No, kisses," and see if she gets it.

Let her chew on some food in your hand while you are petting/touching her to avoid any biting at hands while you are petting, leashing, brushing her. When the petting stops, the food stops.

Use lots of calm and quiet praise with long, calm stroking when she is not biting.

Use something to block her away when she starts the nipping (this is especially good for blocking her away from small kids). My favorite thing is a small cookie sheet; it prevents her from getting to you, and the sound when she makes contact with the metal is often bothersome. Put it like a shield between you or your child (or whatever the target is) and the dog and move toward her as you are blocking. Don't look at or talk to her. Nothing dramatic here; small movements are very effective. Keep it very benign and calm. When she backs away, say "Good dog" and watch to see if she settles. Make sure she is getting lots of attention for stopping her nipping.

DON'T:

Give her attention whenever she wants it. This can cause her to think she can control attention, which can lead to demanding it, which can lead to biting to get that attention.

Use hands as toys. If she grabs you instead of the toy, follow the above pain sound method, then stick the toy in her mouth and reengage.

Roughhouse. It can lead to so many problems.

<u>COME</u>

COMMON BELIEF: *My dog will not come no matter how many times I yell. I have to chase him down, then finally when I get him, I say NO! and drag him home.*

Reverse reality: Gee, I can't imagine why he won't come. The way you describe it, it sounds like so much fun.

Attaching such negativity to the word Come is very common and such a bad idea. Heck, all your dog probably wanted was a good old game of chase. He'll keep going as long as you chase him; when he tires, he'll let you catch him. But berate him when you do catch him, and you can kiss your good Come goodbye.

People tend to use Come only in a formal way, usually attached to ending a dog's fun (come out of the back yard or dog park; come away from the person who's petting you; come over here so I can do something you don't like, say bath, nail trim, ear medicine, etc.). No wonder he goes the other way!

If the dog is running away from you outside, the last thing you should do is chase him (if you do, you are essentially teaching your dog that Come means Go!). You will drive him away from you, possibly into a dangerous situation like traffic. DO NOT CHASE.

Chase is a great game to a dog, so make it work for you – make a lot of noise, clapping, kissing, squeaking a toy, shaking a treat bag – and *run away* from your dog. This will usually get him to reverse course and chase you instead of running away.

Helpful side note: Dogs aren't perfect, which means at some point, no matter how well you have taught Come, your dog will ignore you and keep on going. To keep him safe, you need a backup. For those situations, teach your dog an *Emergency Recall.*

To teach it: Choose an uncommon word that sounds nothing like Come but that you will remember in a panicked state (my dog's is Trouble, but you can use anything: Freeze, Stop, Whoa, etc.). Take some Super

Yummy Treats (think chicken, hot dogs, etc.) and stand in front of your dog. Say the word; treat. Repeat, repeat, repeat, say 30 times. End the session and wait for your dog to wander off to another part of the house. Yell your word and WAIT. See if he comes. If he does, unload a boatload of praise and Super Yummy Treats. Repeat. Train this sparingly but with maximum payoff. So strive for five to 10 repeats a day for a couple of weeks, then every few days, then every once in a while after that. Don't forget to vary the location. Finally, don't overuse it. This is for *emergencies*; if your dog simply isn't coming, go back to working your Come command.

Helpful side note: Do some specific exercises at the front door, gates etc. (Wait is good!) so your dog realizes she should not just dash through any open door. This could be a lifesaver, so don't ignore it!

DO:

Say "Come!" and "Good dog!" every time your dog is heading in your direction to show him how wonderful it is to come to you.

Bring out the biggest rewards you have for Come – top-level treats, play time, car rides, etc.

Start very close to your dog to guarantee a good start, then add distance and distractions.

Enthuse him all the way in from a distance with your voice ("Good dog!") and your body (squat down, throw your arms wide, back up and clap your hands, etc.) so he knows he is doing the right thing.

Use Come for his dinner bowl. Many people use Wait, which is fine, but add a Come!

Also teach an Emergency Recall to use if Come fails

DON'T:

Attach any negatives
Say in anger
Chase

FEAR

Comfort/It's OK

COMMON BELIEF: *When my dog is scared, I can help him deal with that by reassuring him that everything is OK, comforting him with my voice, petting him, holding him till he calms down.*

REVERSE REALITY: You cannot comfort a dog the way you do a human. Dogs associate the reaction you have with the behavior they are currently displaying. When they are displaying fear, "comfort" becomes attention and ultimately, reinforcement of the fear reaction.

Scared dogs need to have the inappropriate reaction (fear) ignored because it needs to extinguish (we are taking away a Precious Thing – attention – that they work hard to get. Give it to them for fear, and you will get more fear.) If you can get them involved in a more appropriate activity (training, play), reward *that* with attention.

If they are too petrified for even that, then ignore them until they calm down. When that happens, since calming down is a desirable behavior, you can reinforce it with attention. CALM attention. No "yappy happy" voice, please.

This lack of reaction on your part is the right way to handle all fear reactions – ignore them as much as possible.

Mild fears then should right themselves quickly (say a startle while walking). The dog sees it doesn't bother you, so they conclude it's not as scary as they first thought. My dog Tawny had a mild reaction to fireworks – the regular sounds didn't bother her, but the loud BOOM at the end of some of the fireworks worried her. So, one Fourth of July, when the show started near our house, and when she got that worried look at the sound of the first BOOM, I turned to her and said, "Wow, what was that? Let's go see!" I walked out into the back yard, and she followed me (important: I didn't force her to come out). After every BOOM, I looked at her and laughed. (Yes, my neighbors all think I'm crazy. For the record, Tawny was looking at me like I was crazy too.) By the end of the show, I'd look at her and laugh, and she looked back and wagged her tail like she was having the time of her life. Done!

Even fear-based aggression needs to be largely ignored, believe it or not. SEE **LEASH/WALKING, OVERREACTIONS, AGGRESSION**.

Helpful side note: Fear can take many forms in dogs: startling, hiding, running away, freezing, cowering, laying down, panting, whining, growling, barking, backing up, snarling, snapping, lunging, biting. Learn to recognize them in your dog so you don't make things worse by correcting a fear reaction. **NEVER CORRECT A SCARED DOG**.

> **DO:**
> *Ignore the fear reaction*
> *Try engaging in another activity (play, training)*
> *Reward attempts by the dog to confront the fear by moving forward, investigating*
> *Stay calm*
>
> **DON'T:**
> *Comfort*
> *Correct*
> *Overreact*

Encouragement/It's OK

COMMON BELIEF: *When my dog is scared, he'll get over it quickly if I force him (nicely!) to deal with it by encouraging forward with lots of happy talk, pulling or pushing him if necessary.*

REVERSE REALITY: This is a technique called "flooding," and it can have really bad and longstanding consequences. I've seen dogs flip over into aggression when being forced in this way (scale in the vet's office, crates). I've seen dogs literally frozen with fear (baths, grooming, vet exams) while owners, thinking they are dealing well with it, are praising away – and when it's over, the dog un-freezes and lashes out. I've seen owners holding dogs in place on leash when the dog is clearly frightened of what is coming toward him, and in a panic to get away tags the owner (see previous *Helpful side note* for examples of the many ways dogs express fear).

Flooding should be avoided at all costs. Careful desensitization is the kindest and most effective way to get past fear.

Example: Plenty of dogs are afraid of the scale in the vet's office. Introduce it the right way by laying down a nice trail of Super Yummy Treats right onto the scale, then lead your dog up to one end of the scale. Then stand there and wait. Eventually, if the treats are good enough, he will walk himself on. Praise calmly, get him off, put the trail back down, and do it again. In short order, he will love the scale!

For fear aggression: See LEASH/WALKING, OVERREACTIONS, AGGRESSION

DO:
*Allow the dog to decide when he
   will confront fear/move forward*
*Motivate by showing Precious
   Things can be earned by moving
   towards fear*
Go slow
Reward with voice
Reward each small step forward

DON'T:
Flood
Force
Encourage with voice

FOOD

Picky eaters

COMMON BELIEF: *My dog is a picky eater, so I have to leave food down all the time so he can eat whenever he likes. I have to constantly try new foods and treats just to find something he likes. I have to do all this so he won't starve!*

REVERSE REALITY: Dogs are opportunistic eaters and should take advantage of what's available when it's available. They usually are not going to starve themselves to death through refusing food they don't care for. Remember, these are the same dogs that will munch on carcasses and dog poop and all manner of unpalatable and unrecognizable things laying around outside. So stop thinking you need to tickle his palate to get him to eat. It's actually more important that food be smelly (they have great noses – see section on treats).

To fix a picky eater, pick up the food. Give him 10 to 15 minutes to eat, then remove the bowl and don't put it down again until the next scheduled meal time. Severely limit or completely eliminate treats temporarily. Eventually, his common sense will tell him he better eat. Of course, if he is crazy stubborn and refuses for several days (highly unusual), then you need to get some groceries into him somehow. But mostly, once he realizes that it is this or nothing, your dog will choose to eat.

Helpful side note: More reasons to not leave food down all the time: dogs can get fat; they can start guarding the food; you may not know if they are off their food; food may become less important, undermining the dog's willingness to do something for you for a treat (aka training).

DO:
Leave food down 10-15 minutes
Limit other food sources (treats, table scraps)
Ignore when food is down

DON'T:
Encourage/plead with/hand feed
Keep trying different foods

Taking food hard/roughly

COMMON BELIEF: *My dog bites my fingers instead of the food! To deal with that, I use a command: "Easy/Gentle/No teeth." Every time he does it wrong, I snatch it away from him and say "Easy" and bring it slowly towards him again, so it's barely within reach (I have to save my fingers!).*

REVERSE REALITY: There is no reason to attach a command to something you want your dog to do all the time. When would you NOT want your dog to take food gently? Whenever food is presented, you want your dog to wait for it to be offered instead of grabbing for it, and take it politely so no one's fingers are ever sacrificed. So forget "Easy" and "Gentle" and all that.

Snatching or holding the food away just increases the frustration level and the likelihood that he will snatch for it (it's going away! Better grab it!) and often makes the situation worse.

Instead, get CLOSER, not farther away. And be quick so he doesn't have time to grab. With a flat hand or fingers, push that treat right into the dog's mouth – he can't possibly snap if you push it into his face. Praise, of course! Another method is to surround the treat with your fingertips and put the back of your fingers right up to the dog's mouth, nearly touching the lips (palm faces down; imagine you are picking something icky off the floor). The dog will investigate to determine where the treat is by nosing around your hand, and when he finds it surrounded by your fingertips, he usually will start licking at it. Sometimes he will stop trying to get at it because he is confused by all those fingers and doesn't want to bite them; he just wants the treat. When he does either one of those two things, turn your hand around, slide the treat into his mouth and tell him how wonderful he is. Then do it again. Once he has the idea, then turn your hand around and bring the treat towards him still surrounded by your fingertips but visible (fingertips pointed at his nose, palm up). Again, wait for him to just nose it or lick it, then release it and tell him he's wonderful.

Doing this helps the dog develop self-control and manners, both of which every dog should have. Some dogs need more work in this area than others. I once worked an old yellow Lab with failing eyesight that was practically ripping people's fingers off in his attempts to get food. (Did I mention he was a Lab?) The rescuers that wanted to put him up for adoption called me in, having thrown up their hands (literally) over this issue. The owner of the rescue told me to bring leather gloves!

Actually, the old boy was pretty easy to fix. But I did have to start the exercise by using my forearm instead

of the back of my fingers (remember, bad eyesight).
I started with the forearm next to his mouth, and my
hand holding a treat was curved away from his face.
Thankfully, he recognized my forearm was not a beef
stick of some kind. I slid my arm along the side of his
head and mouth until the back of my fingers touched
his lips. I turned my fingers and slipped the treat in.
After about 10 minutes, he was no longer Jaws and I
could use my fingers to deliver his treats.

DO:
*Block with the back of your fingers till he stops
   grabbing*
Slip the treat into his mouth quickly
Watch the video clip:
http://www.cp-hipdogs.com

DON'T:
Use a command
Pull your hand away
Yell/get mad

Guarding food

COMMON BELIEF: *So my dog will never guard food, I need to
show her who is boss around the food bowl. I regularly take the
food away when she's eating, then I give it back. I also stick my
hand in the bowl while she's eating, and I pet her while she's
eating.*

REVERSE REALITY: Remind me to never invite you over to my house for dinner.

What you have described is the prescription you would use if you wanted to TEACH a dog how to start guarding his food (or toys, rawhides, etc.). Answer me this: Why should the dog put up with this? Do you liked to be bugged while eating? How would you react if I took *your* plate away midway through a meal? You are messing with her *life-sustaining stuff.* Frankly, I'm surprised when dogs *don't* guard food.

A few years back, I got an emergency call from a family who declared their 18-month-old dog had "suddenly" become food-aggressive, and if I couldn't fix it, the dog might just have to be put down. When I arrived, I met the sweetest thing on four paws; it was hard to believe she was also a "kitchen Cujo." The family insisted it was true, and that she was now even driving the cat away from her empty bowl.

I asked the husband to demonstrate the feeding routine for me. He put a small amount of food in her bowl and walked into the feeding area with it. He asked her to sit and wait, put the food down, then said OK. She started eating eagerly, and he remained standing over her. Then he suddenly reached for the bowl.

Kitchen Cujo appeared with a dramatic snarl and baring of teeth.

"Whoa! Whoa!" I said. "What are you doing?"

The husband replied, "I'm dominating the food bowl."

Sigh.

People, repeat after me: TRUST not dominance. TRUST not dominance. If you are going to ask your dog to allow you to take away her life-sustaining food, you had better have a trusting relationship with her. This family had essentially taught their dog to distrust them with her food, and subsequently other coveted things.

Thankfully, it was an easy fix. I asked for a hot dog cut into little pieces and another bowl of food. As she started eating, I started firing hot dogs in and around the bowl from about 10 feet away as I ambled toward her in my best "I am not a threat" mode. Her tail never stopped wagging, and I was able to stand right next to her without a problem. I told the owners to do the same thing to regain her trust.

DO:

Always BRING something to the bowl – a Super Yummy Treat – and announce you are coming. If you are getting growling from a distance, then toss the food from beyond that distance and slowly move in (sideways, please, and no staring; this is less threatening). If you hear a growl, stop and leave. Try it again later from a distance where you do not elicit a growl, and move more slowly. Variation: Walk by and drop food as you pass. If you hear a growl, keep walking and don't drop the food. Variation: Walk by with second dog on a leash, or cat in a towel.

Practice exchanging the empty bowl for a Super Yummy Treat (use Drop it or Give), then give the bowl back. After doing that for awhile, put a couple of pieces of dog food in the bowl, and exchange some more. This will help her tolerate hands reaching for her bowl.

Put the food down and let her start eating.
Have a Super Yummy Treat in your hand.
Say "Sparky, look what I have!" and wave
the treat to get the dog's attention, then drop
it into the bowl and walk away.

DON'T:

Mess with her food! If you really want to stick
your hands in it, when you do, hand her a
Super Yummy Treat to show her why she
should tolerate such rudeness. Then leave her
alone!

Pet her while she's eating! Again, how would
you like it? If you are afraid little kids will
bother her, besides teaching the kids the right
thing to do and supervising them, DO: Put
the food down and give her a quick stroke as
you walk away. Or bring a Super Yummy
Treat to the bowl, say "Sparky, look what I
have!" and wave the treat to get the dog's
attention, then drop it into the bowl, give a
quick pat and walk away.

GREETING PEOPLE, DOGS

COMMON BELIEF: *My dog is just happy to see me when he*
"goes crazy" when I come home. I love that! It's normal dog
behavior.

REVERSE REALITY: There is nothing normal about this greeting, unless you consider stressed-out, rude, obnoxious and potentially dangerous behavior "normal."

Have you ever seen dogs greet other dogs in this manner? What often happens when they do? They get rebuffed, ignored, snapped at, or worse. That's because it's totally inappropriate and impolite, and most dogs won't tolerate it.

You shouldn't either. If you allow or encourage rudeness in your dog, she will be rude in other ways not as much "fun," and she will be equally rude to others as well. Jumping and hand/clothing grabbing is flat-out dangerous, I don't care how little the dog is. Panting, pacing, barking are all signs of stress.

We have taught our dogs to react this way because it makes US feel good. It's time to check the selfishness and help our dogs calm down. Stress is just as bad for dogs as it is for humans – it shortens the life span.

So give him what he needs. Help your dog relax by ignoring him until he is calm. Then call him to you – CALMLY! – and love him all you want. If he ramps up again, ignore again till he calms. Eventually, you will only get the calm reaction. He's just as happy to see you, but he is reacting in a much healthier, safer way.

Helpful side note: If your dog has got to go potty as soon as you arrive, simply let him out/take him out without talking or eye contact. Once he's back in the house, ignore till calm.

DO:
Reward only a calm, polite greeting
Understand the frantic, stressed-out greeting for what it is
Stay calm when you greet your dog

DON'T:
Encourage this unnatural display
Pay any attention until he's calm

COMMON BELIEF: *When visitors enter my house, my dog is an idiot. She barks/jumps/whines/nips/grabs clothing. I yell, try to distract her, tell her it's OK, but nothing works. I have to put her in her crate.*

REVERSE REALITY: Using the Reverse Principle of giving attention to the behavior you want repeated as a starting point, let's examine what behavior got rewarded here. When your dog is barking/jumping/whining/nipping/grabbing, how much attention is she getting for that? Yelling, it's OK, distracting (Come, Sit, Go to your bed, etc.) + lots of eye contact and physical contact = ATTENTION. "Bad" behaviors reinforced!

DO:

Ring the doorbell repeatedly to desensitize your dog to the sound. When he quiets/calms, praise/treat.

Put a leash on your dog to answer the door. Wave your visitor in, and WALK AWAY from your guest with your dog. Continue walking until he calms down and ignores your guest. Then begin a calm greeting sequence: Walk toward your guest. Any sign of getting excited results in you turning and walking him away. Calmness results in your walking toward your guest. Repeat until you can walk your dog up to the guest, get him to sit, and get him to stay calm and seated while your guest pets him. That's it! Snap off the leash (but be ready to put it back on if he gets excited again. Take off again when calm.).

Develop a great Stay.

Teach a Go To command (Go to your bed/spot/ place etc.) so he will go to a specific place until allowed to come out and greet.

Reward all calm greetings with lots of calm attention! A quiet, polite dog is what you want, so reward when you get it!

DON'T:

Try to talk your dog into being calm

Try to manage him close to guests by saying Off, Sit, Stay, No, etc.

COMMON BELIEF: *Dogs will figure out how to properly greet each other. I just need to let them go and do what they do.*

REVERSE REALITY: While that may be true if humans, leashes and tension weren't involved (and I have my doubts about it even then), it is a dangerous assumption that dogs know how to handle this stuff. A calm, happy, well-socialized dog is one thing, but a dog that is nervous and/or overstimulated and/or frustrated and/or territorial is a disaster waiting to happen, especially if restrained. I've seen dogs that are fine with one another initially get their leashes tangled, and then a fight ensues. I've seen overheated play turn into fights. I've seen a piece of food dropped on the ground turn into a fight. And on, and on, and on. We have shoved dogs into an artificial environment, and it is our responsibility to see they know how to operate in it, and that includes proper behavior when meeting new dogs.

My greeting rules:
- Start outside if possible, and at a distance.
- No dogs greet unless we give permission.
- Walk first, listening to us, and ignoring the other dog.
- Both dogs are calm and polite with each other (this assumes you can read dog body language properly).
- Any impolite behavior results in Precious Things removed, then reintroduced only in the presence of the other dog.
- Both dogs must have a great Leave it-type command so owners can break them up in a heartbeat if need be.

> **DO:**
> *Start outside*
> *Go slow*
> *Watch for tension (stillness bad)*
> *Stay calm*
> *Reward friendly behavior*
> *Move away if growling*
>
> **DON'T:**
> *Tighten the leash*
> *Correct if growling, barking, etc.*
> *Let them "work it out"*
> *Assume if they are OK outside they will be OK*
> * inside*

GROWLING/AGGRESSION

Correcting growling

COMMON BELIEF: *When my dog growls at (a person, a child, a dog, etc.), I have to correct her.*

REVERSE REALITY: You should not correct growling. Growling is a warning your dog is uncomfortable with something. *You want that warning.* If she thinks she is not allowed to growl to let you know she's uncomfortable, then she will go from discomfort to reacting (snarl, snap, bite) with no warning at all.

When I hear growling, my reaction is to figure out what's wrong and do something about it. Generally, I will move the dog away from what she is growling about to bring down the tension till I find out what is going on. If I do that, I usually don't get a stronger reaction, and even if I do, I've moved far enough away that there is no harm done.

Example: I've dealt with many clients who have had their dogs snap at their young children. The biggest mistake the clients make in these situations is they severely corrected the dogs. (Well, actually, the biggest mistake they made was not preparing the dog for the baby before it was born.). Now, the dog believes the baby had something to do with her being severely corrected, which scared her. She's learned that every time the baby is around, bad things happen to her. That should make for some tense exchanges in the near future.

The reverse training that needs to happen here is that, when baby is around, *wonderful* things happen. The best things ever – praise, love, kisses, treats, manna from heaven – but only when baby is around. If you do that every time they are together, how happy is she going to be to see that kid?

Helpful side note: Be sure to train your child, too. They can be taught at a very young age how to be gentle with a dog (and other animals, too).

> **DO:**
> *Recognize growling is an expression of discomfort and a warning you want to have*
> *Move dog away without anger*
> *Fix the problem that caused the discomfort/warning*
>
> **DON'T:**
> *Correct*
> *Panic when you hear a growl*

'Hates' certain people

COMMON BELIEF: *My dog "hates" (men, women, children, certain races, etc.).*

REVERSE REALITY: Dogs generally don't hate anything. But they are surprisingly easy to scare traumatically to the point of developing a fearful and aggressive response to just about anything.

With people, here's what usually happens: Dog spots someone who worries him (e.g. person has a strange walk; he can't see his eyes because he's wearing a cap or sunglasses or a hoodie; he's being loud, shouting; he's making sudden movements; he's riding some contraption like a bike or skateboard). Dog reacts by growling (dog says "I'm uncomfortable"); owner yanks the leash or smacks him and says "Hey!" or No!" in an angry tone. Dog is now more uncomfortable, and the person is getting closer, so his reaction intensifies; he starts pulling/lunging towards the person and barking. The owner's reaction intensifies; stronger corrections ensue. Now the dog is really scared about this person and his reaction shows it. After the person is gone, all the fear goes away too, but the next time he sees that person (or someone like him), he will ramp up again because he has learned bad, scary things happen when he sees that person. Go away, person! he says in Dog.

See **LEASH AGGRESSION/OVERREACTIVITY** for how to fix that.

In your home, the correction can send the dog slinking away, hiding, etc. But the reaction will resurface when the target moves or crosses his path, or gets near his owner or possessions.

To fix that, do NOT ask your guest to give your dog a treat. He's already uncomfortable with the person; don't force him into interacting with him. I've seen a dog go up snarling, take the treat, and go away snarling. Bad idea.

Do the reverse: Put treats in YOUR hand. Move your dog away from the person. See if the dog will take a treat. If he does, have the person move one step closer SLOWLY. Ask the person to point one shoulder toward the dog and look away from him (makes him appear less threatening). As the dog is chewing on the treats, keep the person moving very slowly toward the dog in this angled manner.

Next, stop the person AND stop feeding your dog. Wait a few seconds, then start feeding, and ask the person to slowly move forward again. We want the dog to associate all that great food with the approach of the person. As long as the dog is not reacting to the person, continue. If you get a reaction, stop for the day, and try for a little more next time. The ultimate goal would be to have the person standing near the dog without a reaction. Then allow the person to move a safe distance away (turn away slowly), and stop feeding your dog.

IMPORTANT: Never push your dog past his comfort level. If he reacts, you've gone too fast. Stay calm. Stay SAFE! Use a leash and, if necessary a basket-style muzzle as safety nets.

DO:
Keep treats in your hand
Go slow
Watch for signs of stress in your dog
Stay calm
Stay safe

DON'T:
Have target person interact with dog in early stages
Take chances
Force your dog/push him past his comfort level

HOUSETRAINING

COMMON BELIEF: *When my dog pees in the house I need to 1) tell him NO! 2) smack him 3) drag him to the spot and say NO! 4) put him in his crate.*

REVERSE REALITY: 1) Wrong; 2) wrong; 3) wrong; 4) wrong.

Oh my, if I had a nickel for every housetraining question I've answered over the years.... Owners exhibit a ton of backward thinking when it comes to this problem.

To help you, let's start with this: Understand that housetraining is a totally bizarre concept to a dog. Dogs generally will not go where they eat or sleep. (*Generally* – puppy mill dogs can be a huge exception to that statement, as can hoarders' dogs.) Everywhere else is essentially OK with the dog! You are trying to convince them your entire house falls under this eat/sleep/no-go-here-ever category. A tough concept for many dogs. If you don't watch them like a hawk and catch them every time they wind up to go, you are going to struggle. "Contain" and "monitor" are the two most important words in housetraining.

Dogs learn by experimentation, trial and error. Try it; if it works, keep doing it. If he poops by your bed, and you are not there to interrupt it, he concludes that it is OK to do it when you are not there. You have to catch him every time, interrupt, move him to the right place, praise him if he goes there. Forget the punishment crating afterwards; all you may accomplish there is to make him hate his crate.

Let me say this loud and clear: **YOU CANNOT PUNISH HIM AFTER THE FACT – IF YOU DON'T CATCH HIM, YOU CAN'T CORRECT HIM**. He does not "know what he did," he is reacting to your threatening body language and tone of voice when he looks "guilty" (which is actually appeasement gestures to convince you to stop acting threatening). This is true for every "bad" behavior, by the way.

Helpful side note: Anyone who thinks their dog goes inside for "spite" or "revenge," or that he's being "sneaky," is humanizing unfairly. Sometimes they have a medical issue, sometimes anxiety causes them to lose control. But mostly, it is behavioral, which means housetraining is not done yet.

DO:

Watch like a hawk; tether to you with a leash

Crate/contain if you can't watch (I mean WATCH)

Contain if he doesn't go or completely clean out when given his opportunity

Go out with him, take treats with you, deliver IMMEDIATELY after he finishes (not inside), praise to the rafters, and give him some freedom/fun

Spend time in all rooms to show him proper behavior; take him directly outside from each room to go

Train a potty command: When outside, say it right before he squats ("Want to go out?" when inside the house only means going outside and does not necessarily involve potty time).

Startle/interrupt if he starts to go inside with "uh-uh-uh!" as opposed to stern/scary NO!, then rush him outside to see if he can finish out there.

Clean up any accidents without comment.

> **DON'T:**
> *Punish*
> *Expect a signal until dog is housebroken*
> *Respond to signals until dog is housebroken*
> *Assume trained in your house means trained in all houses*
> *Give them too many chances (like every 15 minutes); they need to develop their hold muscles*

COMMON BELIEF: *While housetraining my dog, I expect him to give me a signal he has to go out.*

REVERSE REALITY: You may grow old and grey, and more than a little frustrated, waiting for that signal. Until he understands he is only supposed to go outside (i.e. is housetrained), why would he give you a signal that he HAS to go outside?

Lots of dogs learn quickly that going to the door, jumping on the owner, and barking at the owner will get the door to open to the outside. That has NOTHING to do with housetraining, and everything to do with them wanting to go outside (aka "doggie Disneyland") and goof around. And yes, maybe pee or poop too.

So essentially, what you are doing is simply giving them the idea they control access to the outside. Be very careful about granting them this power. Dogs that think they control access to the outside may try to control other things as well, and the next thing you know you may have a big old behavior problem on your hands.

When your dog is thoroughly housetrained, then add or expect a signal. Once they know they can't go inside, when they have to go, believe me, they will figure out how to let you know!

So wait till they have it down before you unlock the doggie door, hang up some bells for them to ring, or start to respond to "the look."

Helpful side note: Think pee pads help? Think again. Do you want your dog to ever go in the house? Then why let them? It can be hard to transfer from pee pads to outside – hey, if you had a choice, would you prefer going outside or inside (drunk guys in winter excepted).

If you allow access to the pee pads all the time, you are not really getting your dog to develop his hold-it muscles. If you want to use them all the time (or something similar, like a litter box), you need to limit access to them just like you do outside.

DO:
Housetrain first, then add signal

DON'T:
Assume signal means "I gotta go"

JUMPING

COMMON BELIEF: *My dog is a crazy jumper, so I am saying "No/Off/Down," pushing her down, kneeing her, stepping on her toes, stepping on the leash, turning my back, stepping back, walking away.*

Reverse reality: None of the above work well, and a few are downright cruel.

To stop jumping, do NOT say Off, Down, No or anything else, for that matter. Don't look at her either. Jumping is an attention-getting behavior. She's trying really really hard to get your attention and being really rude about it in the process. So the last thing you want to do is give her what she wants, because that will encourage her to do it again to get more attention.

Jumping is also a rude invasion of your space, and you will not convince her to stop if you move away from her. You gave up space, and she took it. Worked for her.

So reverse what you are doing: Don't look at or talk to the dog. Move toward the jump, whichever direction it's coming from. If you were walking, keep walking in the same direction (be careful not to step on anyone; slide your feet along the floor if necessary to avoid it); if you are standing still, step forward and wait. Eventually she will dribble off of you. When her feet hit the ground, look at her and smile and say *quietly*, "Good girl." She will probably jump again when you do that, so be ready to take attention away and step forward again. Reward with attention when she keeps four feet on the floor. If she stays down through several "Good girls," then squat down to her level and give her some good lovin'. This rewards her well and it often discourages more jumping because you are bringing your face and petting hands down to her level. If she jumps or starts climbing on you, simply stand up and ignore briefly. She should catch on fast and stop what she's doing so she can get you back down there with her.

I've cured many a terrible jumper with this simple technique, including my own dog, Tawny. She used to be 36 pounds of heat-seeking missile whenever I came through the door! Now she jumps on no one.

DO:
Step toward the jump
Ignore
Reward when four are on the floor
Watch the video clip:
http://www.cp-hipdogs.com

DON'T:
Talk
Make eye contact
Push away
Give space/turn, move away
Do anything physical or harmful

LEASH/WALKING, OVERREACTIONS, AGGRESSION

Tight leash, loose leash, and control

COMMON BELIEF: *A tight leash tells my dog I'm in control.*

REVERSE REALITY: A tight leash means you have no control, and you won't be getting any anytime soon.

A tension-filled leash usually enhances reactivity because it transfers tension to the dog. Consider if I grabbed your arm and would not let go, and then started dragging you around by the arm. Would you calmly follow me or smack me to get me to let go? If I kept pulling despite your protests, would you start to panic?

Restraint can be a dangerous thing to a dog – literally, it can be life-threatening (e.g. a leg in a trap or in the mouth of another animal, no access to food or water). A tight leash can have the same stressful impact. They cannot run away from danger if a leash is on them, sometimes causing them to "freak out" (leash frenzy, biting the owner) or go into defensive (charge) mode.

One way guard dogs are taught to attack is to put them on a tight leash and frustrate the heck out of them.

Think about all those things the next time you tighten up on your dog's leash!

I call the leash a "safety net." It's something you use only when necessary. Otherwise, it should be quiet, still and LOOSE.

Helpful side note: Once you have started practicing good walking skills on leash, practice the same exercise off leash inside your home. See if you can get the same results without the leash. That's how to get great walking under all circumstances!

> **DO:**
> *Keep leash loose as much as possible*
> *Use leash only when necessary*
> *Use voice to praise proper behavior*
>
> **DON'T:**
> *Keep leash tight*
> *Steer dog constantly by pulling him around*
> *Chatter constantly at dog to try to get him to go
>   where you want him to go*
> *Only talk when correcting*

COMMON BELIEF: *To get my dog to stop pulling, I yank him back and say No.*

REVERSE REALITY: You will never stop pulling that way. The only time you are giving him feedback is when he is pulling. When he doesn't pull, I bet you ignore him, right? That is totally backwards.

Here's the best basic walking technique I have found.

First, teach your dog to turn back to you whenever he feels tension on the leash:

- Tug (pull and RELEASE) the leash gently to the side, and immediately treat/praise your dog.
- Repeat this until your dog is just watching you, looking for food.
- Next, toss a piece of food away from her, out of leash range. She will follow it and get to the end of the leash. The leash will tighten. When that happens, stand still and WAIT for her to turn back

to you. Keep leash low, still and to the side. Back up slowly if she doesn't turn within a few seconds. When she does turn back, praise/treat.

Now start walking:

- Pay absolutely no attention to any behavior you don't want repeated (jumping, barking, biting the leash, etc.).

- Leash in one hand, treats in the other. Leash is loose (slack), but not so loose the dog is tripping over it. Do not hold the end of the leash only. Fold the excess leash into the palm of your hand and let your arm hang down by your side. Do you see a slight bend to the leash? That's the right amount of slack.

- Step forward. As your dog takes off, stop. The leash will tighten. Back up slowly until she turns toward you. Immediately praise and hand her a treat. Step forward again, and repeat the sequence until your dog is coming back to you the moment she feels the slightest leash pressure.

- Take several steps forward and stop. Your dog should bounce back to you. Immediately turn around (180 degrees), wave a treat at her and walk. She should follow you. Immediately stop and treat. Repeat.

- As you progress, your dog should watch you more and notice you have stopped and turned. Then you can stop turning, add more steps before treating, and add more overall distance. Just remember to stop every time she pulls ahead, and wait for her to come back, back up if she doesn't, then turn in the other direction to get her in position again.

- Acceptable actions by your dog while walking: Quick sniffs of the ground, "air sniffing," looking around, crossing behind owner.
- Not acceptable: Stop and sniff without permission, peeing/pooping without permission, crossing in front of owner, pulling toward anything.

Helpful side note: If your dog likes to start a tug game with the leash, give no attention to that! Don't say Drop it or No. Stop walking. Stick a treat on his nose, and when he drops the leash to take it, say "Good!" DON'T give him the treat but instead lure him forward to start the walking again. After a few steps, stop and treat. Repeat. Or try this: Grab his collar (don't pull!) and drop the leash. Ignore him and wait till he lets go. Say "Good!" Pick the leash up and start walking again. Repeat as needed.

DO:

Teach dog to return to you whenever the leash tightens

Ignore behaviors you don't like

Concentrate on big rewards for proper walking

Keep it fun and lively

Keep it short at first – laps are better than length

Watch the video clip:

http://www.cp-hipdogs.com

> **DON'T:**
> *Yank*
> *Yell*
> *Drag away*
> *Use leash as "brake"*
> *Put the loop end around your wrist (you could
>   get dragged or sprain your thumb/wrist)*

Leash aggression/overreactivity

COMMON BELIEF: *When my dog "blows up" on leash at dogs or humans, I need to strongly correct that. He is being ridiculous, obnoxious, aggressive, and he is embarrassing me! By the way, he's getting worse, so now I only walk him at late at night or early morning.*

REVERSE REALITY: Let's review. Your dog overreacts, so you do too. Then you isolate him to avoid the unpleasantness. Do I really have to tell you why this isn't working?

Ooookay. First, whether he is being aggressive or is simply overstimulated, the last thing your dog needs is more energy added to the situation by you with your strong corrections. He needs a calm example to follow.

Second, isolating a dog with this problem will only make it worse, because to desensitize and modify his behavior, he needs controlled exposures and lots of them. Walking when no one else is around doesn't provide that and only serves to keep that tension level high for both of you (what's that in the distance?!).

Third and extremely importantly: **Most aggression is fear-based.** Correcting a dog when she is afraid is a really bad idea; it just makes her more afraid. That means the reaction gets worse every time you correct. What you need to do is deal with the fear part, not the aggression part.

When you get an overreaction of any kind, your first reaction should be no reaction – no talking, no commands, no shouting of name. Stay calm, turn and walk calmly away from the person/thing causing the reactivity. (Yes, things can cause reactivity too. My dog Tawny has had fear reactions to rocks... you heard me.) Tug-tug-tug gently (not a hard yank) to the side to get and keep your dog moving if need be. Get far enough away that your dog can listen and respond to you, plus take food. Then turn back around, stick a ball of food in front of her nose, and slowly head back toward the fear creator while your dog is munching away.

What?! you say. Go back toward the thing that caused the blow? Yes, that's how you deal with fear/reactivity; avoidance will not fix the problem. If she blows again, turn again and move a little farther away – you went too fast. Wait for her to settle down again (responds to command and takes food), turn toward the scary thing again, put the food ball on her nose again and approach more slowly, taking frequent turn-away breaks (remove food) to prevent more blow-ups.

Hugely important: Don't pay any attention unless she is moving forward (actively confronting her fear). Don't encourage her ("Come on! It's OK," etc.). If she wants to retreat, let her but don't say anything. When she willingly moves forward, munching on her food ball, say "Gooooood giiiirrrrrll" calmly. ONLY TALK TO HER WHEN SHE IS DOING SOMETHING, ANYTHING YOU WANT.

Now you are associating good things with the fear/reactivity inducer, making her less afraid and less reactive.

Helpful side note: Here's a hard thing to hear, but so true: Most aggressive and/or overreactive responses have been taught to dogs (inadvertently, in most cases) by humans. We don't let them retreat when they are nervous; we force them to stay and "deal with it"; we don't show them leadership and in fact make them more scared by overcorrecting them when they are nervous. When that happens, the dog attaches everything around him to that fear experience – whatever dogs, people, etc. were there when he got scared. The next time he sees the things he attached to that intense fear, the reaction he has will be much worse.

DO:
Expose to fear in a controlled way, in small doses dog can handle
Move away from perceived danger to calm and focus dog
Go back towards danger with food
Go slowly so you don't elicit a bad reaction

DON'T:
React to a bad reaction
Correct
Isolate/avoid
Use leash as "brake"
Talk unless dog is moving toward danger and reacting properly

POLITENESS/MANNERS

Impatient for food

COMMON BELIEF: *My one dog is so impatient when I get the food out, so I feed her first.*

REVERSE REALITY: Feed her LAST to teach patience and politeness. She gets nothing until she is quiet and still. Put her behind a baby gate or in her crate if you have to and ignore her till you get polite behavior.

Impatient at the door

COMMON BELIEF: *My dog goes crazy at the door, when I pick up the leash, etc. So I put the leash on and get out the door as fast as possible. Once outside, he's still crazy, so I let him do his thing for a while so he can settle down and walk nice later.*

REVERSE REALITY: If he gets what he wants by acting that way, he will act that way (or worse) forever. So you may need to buy some skates to keep up!

A good walk starts *inside* your house. Calm down the whole leashing process by **not** saying "Sparky! Want to go for a walk? Huh? Huh? A WALK? Yeah? Let's go for a WALK!" If you want him calm and patient, why are you winding him up like that? Then you get mad at him for acting that way, even though you caused it by turning WALK into a trigger word for an overstimulated behavior. (This also applies to RIDE, CAR RIDE, LOOK WHO'S HERE, COOKIE and TREAT, by the way.)

If he goes nuts when you pick up the leash, then pick it up and put it down 1,000 times till he barely reacts to the action. Then ask him to come and sit. Wait till he does both; ignore him till he does. Then start to attach the leash. If, at any point during the leashing process, he pops out of his sit or acts up, stop, stand up and ignore. Don't be afraid to drop the leash and walk away if he won't settle down.

Once leashed, move to the door – *calmly* (if not, return to the leash-up area). Again, the sit must be completed and maintained while the door is opened. The door closes if it is not. Release with an OK, but if he runs through like a fugitive on the lam, bring him back inside and start again at the door. Try again, but this time, back out the door and stand in front of him, one step away. Say Come, make him stop and sit in front of you. Reward him, turn around and move forward into the walk.

DO:
Start a calm walk inside the house
Allot plenty of time to wait for compliance, calmness
Reward whenever calm compliance is shown
Reward with leashing up, door opening, going on walk

DON'T:
Give in to dog's pressure
Talk to calm him or reason with him
Rush to get it all over with

Impatient for attention

COMMON BELIEF: *My dog loves me too much! He will not leave me alone till I say "Go lie down." He pushes my other dogs out of the way, so I have to give attention to all of them at once.*

REVERSE REALITY: You have a rude little dictator on your hands. Be careful! That can lead to other bad behaviors.

Many people think it's cute when dogs come up wagging, pawing, nudging, climbing, etc. That's because dogs look cute when they are doing practically anything. If I walked up to you, sat right next to you, leaned on you and pawed your leg, you would tell me to get lost! Rude, right? Right! And it's also rude when your dog does it to you. If he had opposable thumbs, he would be snapping his paws at you saying "Hey, you, pet me. Hellooo? Pet. Me. Pet. ME. Come on, come on, come on. Again. Again. Again."

Take your power back! Teach your dog some manners. Attention is a Precious Thing you need to control and he needs to earn. Next time he comes up with his demanding cute face, turn your face away and ignore. If he jumps on you, stand up, move toward jump, sit back down. If he flops on your lap, place him back on the ground. IGNORE (that means don't look at him or talk to him). When he gives up, goes away and at last shows some respect, call him over or go to him and give him all the attention you want. Don't be surprised if he ignores *you* when you do!

If he comes up when you are petting another dog, ignore him and block him away from the other dog while you continue to pet the dog you originally were interacting with. Wait for the interloper to go away, and then invite him to join you if and when *you* want him to.

> **DO:**
> *Expect politeness from all your dogs*
> *Ask them to earn your attention by being respectful and responsive*
> *Reward the more polite/patient dog first*
>
> **DON'T:**
> *Talk to or look at a rude interloper*
> *Favor one dog over another*
> *Attempt to be fair in giving attention*

SEPARATION ANXIETY

COMMON BELIEF: *My dog has separation anxiety, so I must spend a lot of time with him and give him more attention to comfort him and let him know I'm there for him and will always come back.*

REVERSE REALITY: If your dog has separation anxiety, he actually needs *less* attention, not more, and the timing of *when* the attention is paid is critically important. Whatever behavior is being exhibited when attention is given is being reinforced. The dog who is constantly begging for attention is being reinforced for that behavior instead of one that would allow him to be calm, relaxed and independent.

Separation anxiety dogs panic when their owners are not around; they are literally addicted to being with the owner, must be with the owner at all times, either because they have been accidentally convinced that they are responsible for the care and safety of the owner, or they cannot exist without the constant attention given them by the owner. When they don't get that attention, they will stress out. One way dogs deal with stress is to chew things. So when your possessions get destroyed, it is not your dog's way of getting even with you for leaving him behind, but rather his attempt to deal with the stress he is feeling. It is an unhealthy and, depending on the level of anxiety, it can be a dangerous existence. Dogs may just wander the house, panting and whining, or they may eat through doors, break their teeth off, rip their nails out, chew holes in themselves and worse.

The way to start fixing it is to not give the dog constant attention (yes, this includes eye contact, talking, even saying the dog's name in passing), and to become very aware of when you give attention so that you are only rewarding calm, polite behavior and not the frantic, stressed ("happy to see me") reactions most owners feed. If you are giving your dog attention every time he demands it (yes, he is being rude and demanding when he comes up to you and puts his nose under your hand, whines, paws, grabs your clothes, jumps on you, etc!), it is time to stop. Ignore him when he does it – turn your head away, gently bump him away, until he goes away and leaves you alone. Then you can reward his good manners with attention, etc.

Helpful side note: Make sure you are actually dealing with separation anxiety and not a medical condition like a urinary tract infection, boredom or a lack of exercise before attempting a fix.

Helpful side note: Separation anxiety can be a tough issue to tackle on your own. You may need a trainer, a behaviorist, a vet, and/or a petsitter to help you. Seek professional help sooner rather than later for this one.

> **DO:**
> *Ignore dog when she is displaying anxious behavior around you*
> *Mark calm behaviors (even laying down and relaxing) with attention*
> *Try busy toys, dog walkers, calming music*
> *Train or retrain dog to happily accept a crate so you have a safe place to keep her*
> *Consult your vet about temporarily medicating if dog is hurting herself*
> *Seek professional help sooner rather than later*
> *Make sure it really is separation anxiety*
>
> **DON'T:**
> *Shower with attention or give attention when the dog demands it*
> *"Spoil"*
> *Punish for destruction*
> *Get another dog to "calm him down"*

STEALING/DROP IT

COMMON BELIEF: *To get something out of my dog's mouth, I chase him down, force it out, then say "No" and take it away.*

REVERSE REALITY: This is a great way to start resource guarding, possibly get bit and possibly cause the dog to hide, destroy or swallow the item. I once had a Cavalier King Charles puppy out of class for awhile because he had gotten the battery out of the remote, and his owners did everything wrong (chased, tried to force), resulting in him swallowing the battery and ending up in surgery to remove it. (He was OK, thank goodness.)

What happened to this dog happens to so many others: So much unpleasantness got attached to letting something go that the goal then became to hang onto that item like grim death. The end result is a lot of misery for both owner and dog.

The fact that dogs taking our things becomes such a national crisis shows our complete lack of understanding of what's going on. All most dogs want to do is start a chase game, and owners teach them that if they pick up certain things, like a sock or shoe, that will do it.

Fixing this problem is easy. One, teach your dog a proper Drop it: Hold treats behind your back. Get your dog interested in a toy. Hold it in your hand and get him to put his mouth on it. When he does, put a treat right on his nose and say "Give" or "Drop it." Wait for him to release the toy. DO NOT pull the item out of the dog's mouth. When he lets go, give him the treat, then give him the toy back. As he gets the idea, start saying "Drop it" while keeping the treat behind your back. Immediately bring the treat to him whether he releases or not (in time, he will.) Progress to tougher objects (special toys, rawhides, empty food bowl), but always make sure you are offering him something that is clearly better than what you want him to give you.

Two, DON'T CHASE. **DON'T CHASE. DON'T CHASE!!** Did I write that enough times? I don't care if that dog has your diamond ring, the real problem starts when you chase. Instead, go to the kitchen and rattle that treat bag. He will usually come running, generally without the item. Go back to the item with your treat and do a formal exchange for the item.

Three, set him up for stealing so he does not take it again. Take whatever your dog likes to pilfer and put it right in front of him. If he heads toward the item to sniff or take, step between him and it, moving forward and blocking with your body and quietly say "No." When he backs away/leaves it alone, praise and/or treat and/or get him involved in something else like training or play. Once he is ignoring the item, return it to its original place and stake it out for awhile to make sure he understands he shouldn't take it no matter where it is (this is experimenting to learn). Make sure you can successfully interrupt him from a distance (sound, water interruptions, etc.). If he looks at it without taking it, walks by or turns away on his own, rain manna from heaven down on him for being so smart. That's how you get him to leave it alone all the time!

My own dog Tawny took everything in the house that wasn't nailed down, so we became well-practiced at this one! Now, everything is safe at our house – even the uncovered wastebasket in the kitchen.

Four, if there is something you cannot tolerate him stealing, *put it away.*

> **DO:**
> *Exchange treat or something better for stolen item*
> *Set up for stealing so he won't take it again*
>
> **DON'T:**
> *Chase*
> *Punish*

YARD BEHAVIOR

COMMON BELIEF: *My dog will be fine out in the yard by himself.*

REVERSE REALITY: Pardon my histrionics, but you are flat-out crazy to leave your dog outside unsupervised. Unless you have a camera attached to the top of his head, you have no idea what trouble your dog might run into in your yard, front or back, fenced or not.

Think I'm being overly dramatic? Here are just the things I have personal knowledge about:

Dogs I know have:
• Run away and never been found
• Been hit by car
• Been attacked by other animal or attacked/killed another animal
• Been skunked
• Destroyed property including expensive landscaping, furniture, outbuildings, fencing through chewing, digging, looking for something to play with

- Jumped over the fence, dug under the fence, chewed through the fence, broken through electric fences
- Terrorized dogs on walks by charging, lunging, banging against fences, following, menacing, barking, snarling

And this is just dogs *I* know!

Your yard is not a playpen with only safe toys inside; it is not a babysitter. You need to teach your dog how to behave in your yard just like you would any other room of your house. You need to teach him how to act with a fence, conventional or electric. if you are allowing your dog to charge the fence, you are being irresponsible and – bonus – you are setting up your own dog for a stupendous fall if he ever breaks out because all that pent-up anxiety can be unleashed on the dog or human when he finally gets to the source of his frustration. A client who came to me after his dog bolted out of a car and killed another dog still would not take my advice and do the work necessary to fix this problem in his otherwise lovely Lab mix, and had to have her euthanized when she got out again and attacked another dog. Heartbreaking and totally avoidable.

Another person became a client after she nearly choked the life out of her Husky when she was charged by a dog in a yard. The client was afraid her dog would hurt the smaller dog, and she ended up crushing her dog's trachea.

I myself have been charged more times than I can count, and I have gone from being worried about my dog, the charging dog and myself, to being really angry at the owners who should not be putting their dogs in such a position.

And for those of you who say your dog stays in the yard "most of the time": I do not want to be around when you have that one catastrophic failure. And by the way, your neighbors are sick of retrieving your dog, calling you to retrieve your dog, having your dog pee and poop in their yards, chasing your dog off, getting charged and/or barked at by your dog, etc. Frankly, you are making us all look bad and putting your dog and everyone else at risk.

Okay, cleansing breath... Tirade over. Now here's some help.

DO TEACH:

Barrier respect: How to stay away from the fence, not charge it/jump it/dig under it, etc.

What to touch/not touch (what can he play with)

What to do when someone approaches

What to do when someone walks by, with or without a dog

Where to dig if need be

Come, Leave it, Enough/Quiet, Down, Stay

DON'T:

Leave him alone outside forever! For Pete's sake, bring him in. Dogs are social animals; isolating them is one of the worst things you can do!

***

FINAL REALITY

COMMON BELIEF: *This is too much work!*

REVERSE REALITY: What is really too much work is all you have to do to deal with your dog when you can't or won't put in the work you need to at the beginning. Working to train a dog properly for the first year or two of her life with you will get you 10, 12, 15 or more years of well-behaved dog. Don't do that work, and you end up with 10, 12, 15 or more years of "bad" dog which is a lot more work plus it causes a lot more stress and grief. So buckle down and do it NOW so you can relax and enjoy your wonderful pooch!

Helpful side note: You can do it if you believe you can. I believe you can!

DO:
The work!

DON'T:
Give up!

Index

21506919R00060

Made in the USA
San Bernardino, CA
03 January 2019